THE EXTRAORDINARY LIFE OF

GRETA
THUNBERG

PUFFIN BOOKS

UK | USA | Canada | Ireland | Australia
India | New Zealand | South Africa

Puffin Books is part of the Penguin Random House group of companies
whose addresses can be found at global.penguinrandomhouse.com.

www.penguin.co.uk
www.puffin.co.uk
www.ladybird.co.uk

First published 2020

002

Text copyright © Devika Jina, 2020
Illustrations copyright © Petra Braun, 2020

The moral right of the author and illustrator has been asserted

Text design by Perfect Bound Ltd
Printed and bound in Great Britain by Clays Ltd, Elcograf S.p.A.

A CIP catalogue record for this book is available from the British Library

ISBN: 978-0-241-44389-7

All correspondence to:
Puffin Books
Penguin Random House Children's
One Embassy Gardens, New Union Square
5 Nine Elms Lane, London SW8 5DA

MIX
Paper from
responsible sources
FSC® C018179
www.fsc.org

Penguin Random House is committed to a
sustainable future for our business, our readers
and our planet. This book is made from Forest
Stewardship Council® certified paper.

THE EXTRAORDINARY LIFE OF
GRETA
THUNBERG

Written by Devika Jina
Illustrated by Petra Braun

EXTRAORDINARY LIVES

PUFFIN

World Map

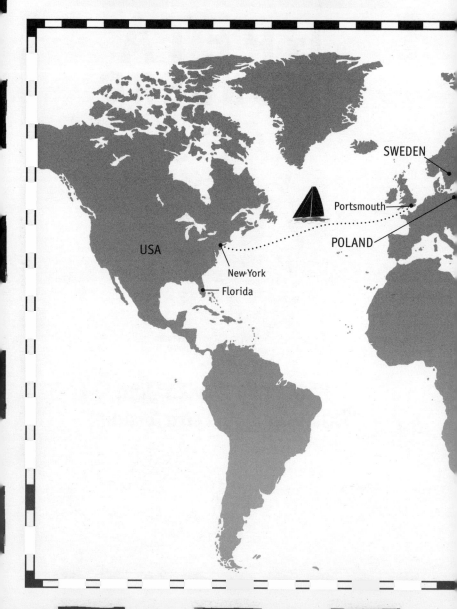

SWEDEN

Portsmouth

USA

POLAND

New York

Florida

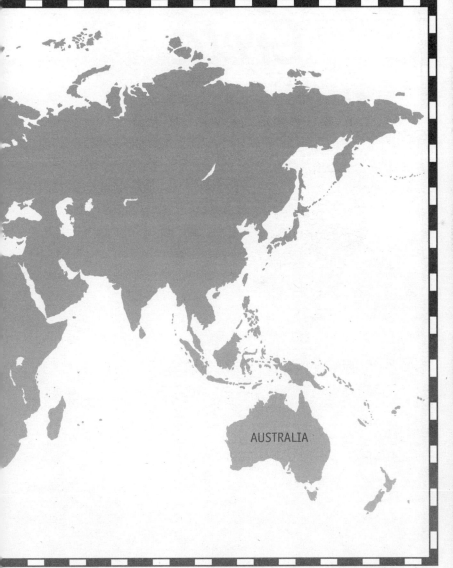

AUSTRALIA

WHO IS
Greta
Thunberg?

Greta Thunberg

was born in Stockholm, Sweden,
on 3 January 2003.

*B*y the time she celebrated her ***sixteenth birthday*** she had made it her mission to help solve the global climate crisis. Now Greta is known everywhere for her bravery, conviction and commitment, and she continues to show the world just how much one young woman can do. Greta was only ***eight years old*** when she first learned about the problem of climate change, and since then she has been ***fiercely determined*** to solve it.

For years it *frustrated* her and made her angry. She even stopped talking and eating. But eventually she realized that even a young girl could **make a difference**.

On 20 August 2018 Greta made her way to the RIKSDAG to tell her country's leaders that they needed to do more to **protect the planet** and the future of young people like her. It wasn't long before people started paying attention.

RIKSDAG: the Swedish equivalent of the UK's Houses of Parliament.

Whatever she faces, Greta refuses to be held back from **achieving her goal** – getting those in charge to do more to solve the climate crisis. Sometimes people have picked on her or called her names just because she's **different** from them.

Once a solitary schoolgirl sitting outside Swedish Parliament to **make a stand**, Greta went on to inspire a global climate STRIKE and now has **millions of people** of all generations listening to what she has to say, and pushing for positive change because of it.

STRIKE:
a group of people on strike refuse to go to school or work in order to protest for a greater cause.

SKOLSTREJK
FÖR
KLIMATET

This is the *story of the might* and courage of a teenage girl. Already Greta has showed just what a determined young person can do to make the world a *better place*, and this is only the beginning.

This is the story of Greta Thunberg, the girl who got the whole world to listen.

Growing up

Greta's early life was pretty ordinary. She was born on 3 January 2003 and raised in Stockholm by her mother, *Malena*, and father, *Svante*. Malena Ernman was a celebrated opera singer and Svante Thunberg was an actor and author.

Greta had a normal childhood – going to school and playing with her little sister Beata.

She went to school every day, read books and did her homework.

Greta first learned about climate change in 2011, when she was eight years old. Her teachers showed her class some *documentaries*, and explained what was happening.

Climate change

This term is used to describe any significant long-term change in the weather patterns of a region or the whole planet. Recently we use it to describe the steady rise in temperature of the Earth's surface, known as global warming. The Earth is getting warmer and warmer every year, at a rate that is much faster than anything we've seen before. Many people believe that the effects of modern global warming are a direct result of human activity like burning FOSSIL FUELS, pollution and deforestation. The true scale of humanity's impact on the Earth is yet to be seen, but either way climate change presents a very real and topical problem.

FOSSIL FUELS:
the three fossil fuels are petroleum (oil), coal and natural gas, all of which are the remains of organisms that lived millions of years ago. Burning fossil fuels provides about ninety per cent of the energy needed to run modern machines.

'The first time I heard about

GLOBAL

WARMING

I thought:

THAT CAN'T BE RIGHT.

No way there is something

SERIOUS

enough to threaten our very

EXISTENCE'

In Greta's classroom, images of rising sea levels, cyclones, heatwaves and so much more swept across the screen. They were **shocking**, but far away from the Stockholm classroom she was sitting in.

The class ended and everyone seemed to carry on with life as normal. But Greta **couldn't forget** what she had seen. Those images were locked at the front of her mind, and she needed to know what could be done to fix the problem.

'Our teachers showed us films of

PLASTIC

in the ocean,
starving polar bears and so on.

I CRIED

through all the movies.
My classmates were concerned
when they watched the film, but
when it stopped, they started
thinking about other things.

I COULDN'T DO THAT.

Those pictures were stuck
in my head.'

The climate crisis

Greta could see the huge scale of the problem, and it scared her. She couldn't understand how our world leaders weren't scared like her, and why they weren't doing more to **protect** the planet we call home.

There's still time to fix global warming, but quick and well-considered actions are needed.

Greta felt completely *powerless*. What could she do to make things better? She had no answers, and by 2014 that *overwhelming* feeling of sadness and dejection became a daily reality.

She stopped talking, refused to eat, and spent more and more time alone, *shutting herself off* from her family. Seeing this change in their daughter, Greta's parents became increasingly worried about her. They took her to appointments with doctor after doctor in the hope that they might be able to work out what was happening.

Eventually, after many tests and questions, Greta was diagnosed with depression. She was twelve years old.

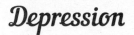

Depression

Depression is a mental condition that can make the sufferer feel sad, frustrated, discouraged or irritated. Someone with depression can feel like this for days, weeks, months or years, but there are always ways to help.

Slowly but surely Greta *opened up* to her parents. She explained that the reason for her sadness and anger was that people in charge were doing little to address the problem of climate change. How would things get better? How could she, a child, do something to make a difference?

Greta has Asperger's syndrome, a lifelong condition that can cause social anxiety, making interacting with others very difficult. People with Asperger's often develop a very focused and particular fascination or fixation on a particular subject, and can notice tiny details.

Greta acknowledges that having Asperger's syndrome makes her seem different to some other people. But she doesn't shy away from a challenge. Greta talks about her Asperger's as openly as she does about the future of our planet, and she thinks of it as a blessing. She has used something often described as a barrier as an opportunity.

'It makes me see things from OUTSIDE THE BOX. I don't easily fall for LIES. I can see through things. If I would've been LIKE EVERYONE ELSE, I wouldn't have started this SCHOOL STRIKE.'

Greta started reading and learning more about climate change, which she calls a **climate crisis**. If she was going to crack this puzzle, she was determined not to lose focus.

She studied the science and went to marches and RALLIES whenever she could.

RALLY: a mass meeting of people showing support for a particular cause.

She wanted to pick apart the problem in front of her and do *something* to make the situation better.

Every word she read added fuel to her determination, and every statistic she learned gave her even more knowledge that she could apply to her cause. She quickly started ***making changes*** to her own lifestyle, seeing that she had a ***responsibility*** to care for the planet. She stopped eating meat and cycled or walked whenever she could.

The meat-eating industry is estimated to be responsible for anywhere between fourteen and eighteen per cent of human-caused GREENHOUSE GASES, because of the amount of fossil fuels that are burned and the land that is cleared to keep livestock.

Soon her parents followed suit, and her mother gave up flying.

GREENHOUSE GASES: gases in the atmosphere that trap energy from the sun. These cause the Earth's surface and air to warm.

' She kept showing us

DOCUMENTARIES,

*and we read books together.
Before that, I really didn't*

HAVE A CLUE.

I thought we had the

CLIMATE ISSUE

sorted .'

– Svante Thunberg, Greta's father

Seeing how much conviction their daughter had, Malena and Svante couldn't help but **admire** how far she had come. Not so long ago she wasn't eating or speaking – but soon she would be a force to be reckoned with.

'There was

NO HINT

of this in her childhood.

IT'S UNBELIEVABLE.

If this can happen,
anything can happen.'

– Svante Thunberg

These were the early signs of a trailblazer in the making, and it wouldn't take long before the whole world could see it.

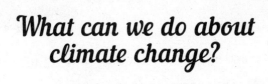

What can we do about climate change?

Not everyone can walk or cycle everywhere, and we can't all grow more plants for food. So what else can we do? Everything makes a difference, like using a reusable water bottle or recycling. Can you think of other ways you can help the environment every day? We may not be making decisions on the world stage, but as Greta learned no one is too small to make a difference.

What is at stake?

Why are millions of people standing up to push our leaders to do more to combat climate change? Greta talks about a report by the IPCC a lot, and although it's a heavy read it's an important one.

It tells us that the Earth has warmed to three degrees above PRE-INDUSTRIAL levels and this isn't good for us or the planet.

PRE-INDUSTRIAL: the time before humans discovered fossil fuels.

As a result we see more ***extreme weather***, like floods, droughts, cyclones and forest fires. Nearly 200 species of plants and animals become extinct every day due to global warming. None of this is happy news, but the good news is that there is still time to act. As Greta says, we need our leaders, businesses and ordinary people to come together and work towards the same goal.

What is the IPCC?

It's the Intergovernmental Panel on Climate Change, which was set up in 1988 by a man named Bert Bolin. It's the department of the United Nations dedicated to studying the science behind climate change, and it brings governments together to work out how to address the issues we're seeing as a result of global warming.

As well as learning about the problem Greta wanted to find out how to help solve it. It was at this time that Greta discovered **activism**, and how it had brought about positive change in the past. Learning from the people she met on marches, and those living in other countries, Greta began to see a way out of the mess those in charge had created.

What is an activist?

Someone who campaigns for or educates others to bring about positive change in the world. They might do this by encouraging lifestyle changes, speaking up about an issue to raise awareness, or bringing like-minded people together to hold protests or marches.

Thousands of miles away from Greta's home in Stockholm, a group of American teenagers were getting ready to march to Washington DC. Like her they were *furious* with the people in charge, and they were preparing to tell them why.

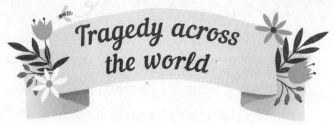

Tragedy across the world

On 14 February 2018 in Parkland, Florida, a teenager walked into Marjory Stoneman Douglas High School with a gun. He opened fire on the students. Seventeen people died and seventeen more were injured. Others ran and hid around the school, waiting for it to end.

Among the survivors was Cameron Kasky, who, along with some of his classmates, announced that he would not go to school any more. Instead they would **protest** and march along PENNSYLVANIA AVENUE.

PENNSYLVANIA AVENUE:
the road that connects the White House, the home of the US president, to the Capitol, the home of the US Congress.

Exactly a month after the shooting, Cameron, his classmates and thousands more young people in America **took to the streets**, and so the 'March for Our Lives' movement was born.

STOP

PROTECT KIDS

NO GUNS

ENOUGH

What does the US Congress do?

The Congress makes laws for the country, and its members are elected by the American people. Members of Congress vote on bills or proposed laws before they can be passed to the president and signed into law. They work in the Capitol, which is down the road from the White House.

They took to one of the most important streets in America to protest gun laws in their country, which they argued needed to *change*. How could it be so easy for someone to walk into a school and open fire? This was wrong, and they wanted to see their leaders do something to stop it and protect the lives of children and young people. That was part of their job, after all.

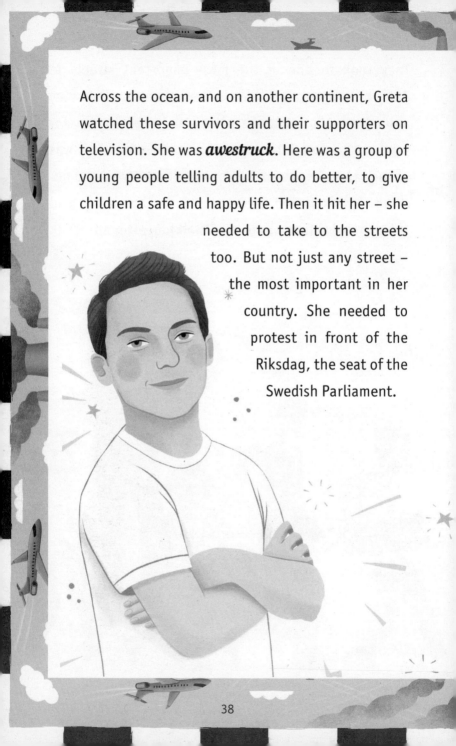

Across the ocean, and on another continent, Greta watched these survivors and their supporters on television. She was **_awestruck_**. Here was a group of young people telling adults to do better, to give children a safe and happy life. Then it hit her – she needed to take to the streets too. But not just any street – the most important in her country. She needed to protest in front of the Riksdag, the seat of the Swedish Parliament.

Just like Cameron Kasky and those standing shoulder to shoulder with him, Greta decided she wouldn't go to school. Instead she was going to protest to make people see the need to act for the *future of our planet*. She would do this until the people in charge took *real action*.

The Swedish general elections were coming up, and Greta wanted to make sure that politicians were keeping the climate crisis at the front of their minds. There had been a worrying number of wildfires and heatwaves across Sweden, and Greta didn't see her country's government doing anything to address them. So she decided to *strike every day* until the elections closed on 9 September 2018. She was ready.

What is a general election?

A vote by the citizens for the leaders of a country. Leaders of different political parties present the changes they want to make over a series of TV appearances, speeches and meetings with the public in an effort to show them how they can make the country and their lives better. This goes on for several months, and then the vote opens to adults living in the country. At the end of the voting period the results are counted and the person or party with the most votes becomes the next leader. In Sweden this process happens every four years.

VOTE

Greta immediately asked her classmates for help. It turned out that they were worried about climate change too, but *skipping school* was something they didn't want to do. They knew they'd get into trouble. So while they supported Greta she soon learned that she'd be striking alone. Her parents weren't happy about her decision either.

'When I told my parents about

MY PLANS

they weren't very fond of it.
They did not support the idea of

SCHOOL
STRIKING

and they said that if I were to
do this, I would have
to do it completely

BY MYSELF.'

A scary thought, sure, but she wasn't going to back down. Little did Greta know that that Friday morning in August was about to start a global movement, millions strong, which would end up being louder than she had ever imagined.

'Why should I be studying
for a future that soon may

BE NO MORE,

when no one is doing anything to

SAVE THAT
FUTURE?

And what is the point
of learning facts when the
most important facts clearly mean

NOTHING TO OUR
SOCIETY?'

Striking for change

On the morning of Monday 20 August 2018 Greta woke up, brushed her teeth and ate her breakfast. But instead of getting ready for school, she took hold of her hand-painted banner emblazoned with the words 'Skolstrejk för klimatet'.

The banner translates as 'school strike for the climate'.

SKOLSTREJK FÖR KLIMATET

She walked out of the front door and made her way to the Riksdag.

Alone but unfazed, Greta sat down and started her solo strike.

Sitting cross-legged, she laid her sign out, and put a stone on top of a pile of flyers about climate change to stop them from blowing away in the wind. She had what she needed to start, but now she needed people to *pay attention*.

'I painted the sign on a

PIECE OF WOOD

and, for the flyers, wrote down

SOME FACTS

I thought everyone should know.
And then I took my bike to the

PARLIAMENT

and just sat there . . .

I SAT ALONE

from about 8.30 a.m. to 3 p.m. -
the regular school day.'

True to her word, Greta made the journey every morning. She sat down outside the Riksdag with her banner in front of her, defiant, determined and *focused on her goal*. She was striking so that others would pay attention, and it didn't take long for them to listen.

'On the

SECOND DAY

people started

JOINING ME.

After that there were

PEOPLE

there

ALL THE TIME'

One of the people who joined her was a man named *Ingmar Rentzhog*. He had heard about the young girl sitting outside the Riksdag instead of going to school, calling on her leaders to take positive action for the climate. Intrigued by her motivations and wanting to support her, Ingmar made his way to where she sat.

The image of Greta alone on the pavement struck Ingmar immediately. He had three children and it really resonated with him when he saw Greta calling on 'grown-ups' to do something for the future of the planet. He wanted to help her. So he walked to where she sat and said *hello*.

Did You Know?

Ingmar is the founder of a social media platform called 'We Don't Have Time.' He set it up to bring together people from across the world and enable them to talk about how to make a positive change to our planet and global society. It's no wonder then that Greta's strike caught his attention!

After speaking to her for a while Ingmar asked Greta if he could take a photo of her with her sign and post it to **Facebook**. His post was emotional and pushed for people to go to the Riksdag to meet Greta and speak to her.

'Make a

HEROIC EFFORT.

Go by the parliament.
Talk to

GRETA

and show she's

NOT ALONE ...

She needs your support now!'

– Ingmar Rentzhog

It worked. 14,000 people reacted to the post, and almost six thousand people shared it so others could see it. Greta tweeted it too, spreading the word further.

Greta's solo strike continued every day, just as she had promised. And on 7 September 2018 she went even further. Greta announced that she would continue the strike *every Friday* until the Swedish Government committed to reducing their carbon emissions, as set out in the Paris Agreement of 2015.

We live in an age where social media connects us with each other and allows us to talk about important issues like climate change, and Greta's story shows how *powerful* this can be. The image of a fifteen-year-old girl, hair in plaits, cross-legged outside the seat of the Swedish Parliament spread far and wide. Soon Greta wasn't alone any more – *millions more* in hundreds of countries across the globe joined her. And so the #FridaysForFuture movement was born.

Paris Agreement

The Paris Agreement was signed by businesses and governments across the world to show their commitment to keeping the global temperature rise well below 2 degrees Celsius, and to push for an increase below 1.5 degrees Celsius. After signing, however, some countries, like the United States, wanted to pull out, as President Donald Trump claimed that the agreement was an unfair set-up that was damaging the US economy. This makes it even more important that people across the globe continue to push for change.

#FridaysForFuture

#FridaysForFuture was started by Greta, and soon after there were other young climate activists who began setting up marches in their hometowns.

On 30 November 2018 around fifteen thousand school children in thirty cities up and down Australia followed Greta's lead and took to the streets.

RAISE
YOUR
VOICE
NOT THE
SEA LEVEL

DON'T
BE A
FOSSIL
FOOL

FIGHT
FOR A
FUTURE

OUR
FUTURE
YOUR H

CLIMATE
CHANGE
IS REAL

WE CAN MAKE A
DIFFERENCE

Not everyone was happy about it. Only a few days earlier, while the students were ready and waiting to strike, the Australian prime minister Scott Morrison told the Australian Parliament:

'What we want is

MORE LEARNING

in schools and

LESS ACTIVISM.'

NDS

NO FOREST
NO FUTURE

I'D BE IN SCHOOL
IF THE WORLD
WERE COOL

WE ARE RUNNING
OUT OF TIME

This particular strike had been started by Harriet O'Shea Carre and Milou Albrecht, who wrote to other young Australians like them, asking for their support:

'JUST GOING TO SCHOOL *isn't doing anything about* CLIMATE CHANGE. *And it doesn't seem that our* POLITICIANS *are doing anything, or at least* NOT ENOUGH, *about climate change either.'*

And the revolution was spreading. More and more young people were making signs and marching in the hope that finally their leaders would *pay attention*.

A month later, in early December 2018, preparations were almost finished for the United Nations Climate Change Conference in Katowice, Poland. Knowing that political leaders were getting ready to discuss the burning issue, millions more young people made *preparations* of their own. In the lead-up to the conference, and during it, strikes were organized in 270 cities across the globe, from Belgium to Japan.

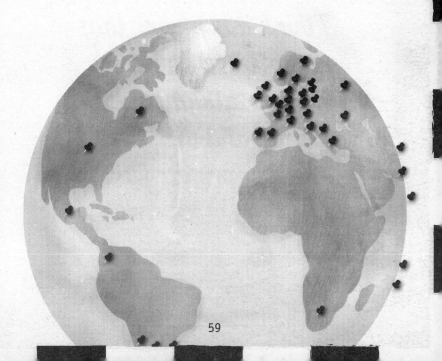

Meanwhile Greta had been **invited to speak** at the conference. She thought it was funny that the people she was calling on to act had invited her to speak about a problem that they weren't doing enough to resolve.

'*I think it is insane that people are gathered here to talk about the climate and they arrive here in private jets.*'

On 15 December 2018 she took to the stage and looked out at the crowd. Here, in the same room as her, were the people Greta held responsible for the future of the planet and who had the power to do something about it. They watched and listened to her intently, and she did not hold back from telling them how and why they needed to act urgently.

'The year 2078; I will celebrate my seventy-fifth birthday. If I have children, maybe they will spend that day with me. Maybe they will ask me about you. Maybe they will ask

WHY YOU DIDN'T DO ANYTHING

while there still was time to act. You say you love your children above all else, and yet you are

STEALING THEIR FUTURE

in front of their very eyes.'

Hers was a SENTIMENT shared by millions more young people around the world.

SENTIMENT:
a view or
opinion.

The #FridaysforFuture movement kept on growing, and, within only a year, there were thousands of strikers in hundreds of cities.

On 15 March 2019 the first ever #FridaysForFuture *global strike* was held. 1.4 million young people in 2,000 countries grabbed hold of their placards and signs emblazoned with battle cries in their own languages.

Like Greta on that first August morning, they refused to go to school until their leaders **_took action_**. History will never forget how powerful Greta looked the day she sat outside the Riksdag. Now she knew she wasn't alone.

#FridaysForFuture continued every week, with strikes across the globe and the hashtag trending across social media most Fridays.

Greta has millions supporting her, and politicians hang on to her every word as she tells them to do better. But for someone so young she has also faced her share of BACKLASH.

BACKLASH: a strong negative reaction by a large number of people.

Some people call her names and focus only on what makes her different, rather than looking at the importance of what she's saying and the urgency of the situation we're in.

Ever focused and determined, Greta doesn't falter, though. Making it clear that her Asperger's and horrible comments won't hold her back, Greta remembers a time before she started the climate strike, when she had no motivation to do anything, or speak to anyone.

'I just sat alone at home, with an

EATING DISORDER.

All of that is gone now, since I have found a

MEANING

in a world that sometimes seems

MEANINGLESS

to so many people.'

Her supporters have challenged those who poke fun at her, saying that it is because of ABLEISM.

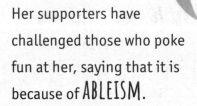

ABLEISM: discrimination against someone with a disability or long-term condition.

'When haters go after your looks and differences it means they have nowhere left to go and then you know

YOU'RE WINNING!

I have

ASPERGER SYNDROME

and that means that sometimes I'm a bit different from the norm, and given the right circumstances being different is

A SUPERPOWER.'

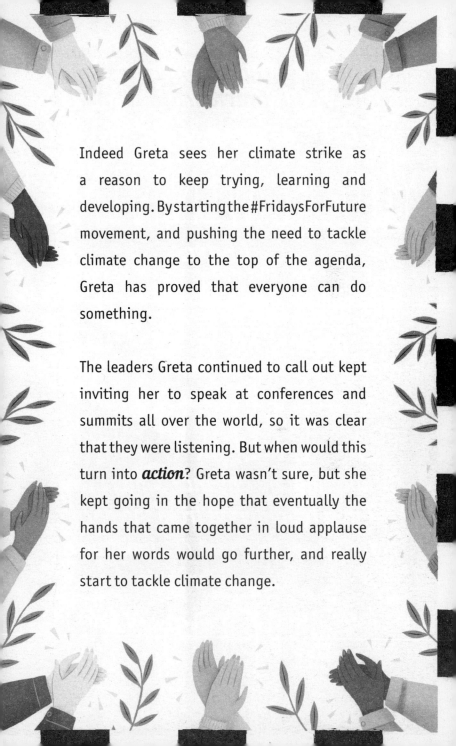

Indeed Greta sees her climate strike as a reason to keep trying, learning and developing. By starting the #FridaysForFuture movement, and pushing the need to tackle climate change to the top of the agenda, Greta has proved that everyone can do something.

The leaders Greta continued to call out kept inviting her to speak at conferences and summits all over the world, so it was clear that they were listening. But when would this turn into *action*? Greta wasn't sure, but she kept going in the hope that eventually the hands that came together in loud applause for her words would go further, and really start to tackle climate change.

A carbon-neutral journey

Greta was invited to speak at the United Nations Climate Summit in New York. But how was she to get there?

Aeroplanes use a lot of energy, and a journey from Plymouth to New York would burn around 986 kg of carbon dioxide for each passenger – more than most people use per year in fifty-six countries around the world. Greta had long ago decided to stop flying, so she needed to find another way of getting to the summit.

Luckily she was contacted by the captain of the *Malizia II*, a **high-speed boat**. But this was no ordinary boat. At 18.2 metres long it was covered in solar panels across the roof and non-slip panels on the top, so Greta and the rest of the crew could walk on them without falling.

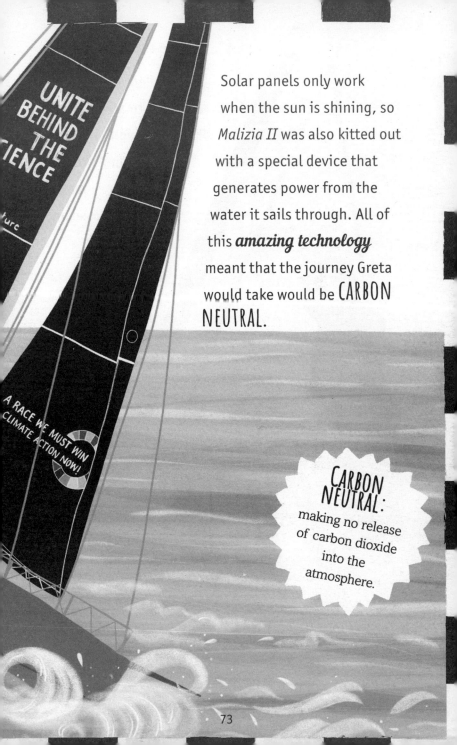

Solar panels only work when the sun is shining, so *Malizia II* was also kitted out with a special device that generates power from the water it sails through. All of this ***amazing technology*** meant that the journey Greta would take would be CARBON NEUTRAL.

CARBON NEUTRAL: making no release of carbon dioxide into the atmosphere.

UNITE BEHIND THE ~IENCE

A RACE WE MUST WIN CLIMATE ACTION NOW!

Greta sailed with captain Boris Herrmann, skipper Pierre Casiraghi, her own father, and Swedish documentary-maker Nathan Grossman.

A carbon-neutral boat is pretty cool, right? It is, but Malizia II doesn't have a toilet, shower, kitchen or any privacy. But Greta knew it was the right decision and didn't mind that at all. She was happy sailing for fourteen days across the Atlantic.

After setting off from London on 14 August 2019, she kept the public up to date with her voyage. As you can imagine sailing across a massive ocean during hurricane season with four other people on a small boat could be a little **difficult** to say the least, but that didn't stop the fun, or alter Greta's reasons for doing it.

On Day 4 of her two-week-long journey she said:

'Eating and
sleeping well and

NO SEASICKNESS

so far.

Life on

MALIZIA II

is like camping on a

ROLLER COASTER!'

And so the voyage went on, until she arrived in **New York City** on 28 August 2019.

Greta climbed off the boat at North Cove Marina at the southern tip of the city and stepped on to dry land. She was greeted by large groups of people. They had come to cheer her on and let her know that she wasn't alone – they all wanted climate action too.

She addressed the crowd with a clear and confident message.

'We need to stand together and

TAKE ACTION

because otherwise it might be

TOO LATE.

Let's not wait any longer.

LET'S DO IT NOW.'

Greta's journey to New York was timely. As she stepped off *Malizia II* preparations were underway for two of the biggest and most **momentous** events of their kind – the first Global Climate Strike and the United Nations Climate Summit.

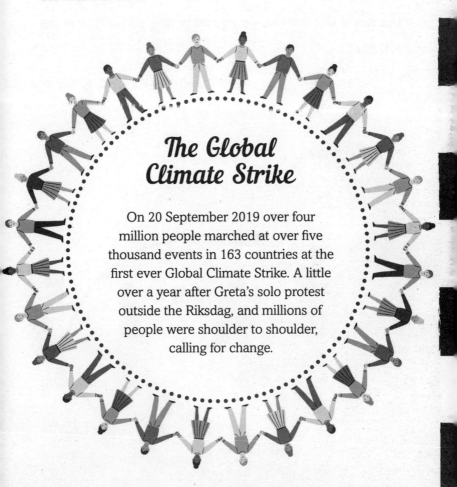

The Global Climate Strike

On 20 September 2019 over four million people marched at over five thousand events in 163 countries at the first ever Global Climate Strike. A little over a year after Greta's solo protest outside the Riksdag, and millions of people were shoulder to shoulder, calling for change.

On the day of the Global Climate Strike Greta addressed a crowd of millions in New York City. Stepping on to the podium, she was a symbol of the might, determination and calm that she has come to be celebrated for. In Greta we see a young woman who knows what she wants from the world she lives in, doing *everything she can* to make it better.

'We have not taken to the streets, sacrificing our education, for the adults and politicians to take selfies with us and tell us that they really, really admire what we do.

We are doing this to

WAKE THE LEADERS UP.

We are doing this to get them to act. We deserve a safe future, and we

DEMAND A SAFE FUTURE.

Do you think they hear us?'

Greta marched that day, along with the millions who have rallied alongside her since that August 2018 morning. A mass of young people calling on our leaders on the streets of New York is something that has happened many times, but this time it was a little different. Everyone was thinking about the meeting that was to open the following day.

OUR
FUTURE
MATTERS

GO
GRETA

WE NEED
CHANGE

CLIMATE
JUSTICE

SAVE
OUR
PLANET

The United Nations Climate Summit

The United Nations Climate Summit was called by the UN secretary general António Guterres in late 2018, after it became clear that efforts to tackle climate change weren't enough to get the planet through it. There are plenty of summits that bring world leaders together to discuss how they can make a positive change for people and the planet, but António Guterres wanted this one to be different. The only leaders who would speak would be those who had a plan to keep global warming to or below 1.5 degrees Celsius. The hope was that this meeting would result in some clear actions our leaders could take.

OUR
FUTURE
IN
YOUR
HANDS

THE CLIMATE
IS CHANGING,
WHY AREN'T
WE ?

ACT
NOW

CLIMATE
CHANGE
IS REAL

ON
FIRE

OUR

By this point Greta and others like her had grown **tired** of political leaders giving praise and applause to young climate activists, because they didn't see this translating into the necessary action. That same frustration Greta had felt when she had first learned about the massive issue crept back, but this time it *pushed her* to keep fighting.

Another podium to step on, another microphone to lean in to, as she delivered another speech. Greta looked out at the crowd, and told the awe-struck faces in front of her:

'This is all

WRONG.

*I shouldn't be up here.
I should be back*

IN SCHOOL

*on the other side of the ocean.
Yet you all come to us*

YOUNG PEOPLE
FOR HOPE?'

Enough was enough. Leaders said they were listening. They were inviting her to speak. But now she wanted to see them do something. What was it going to take?

'We don't want to be INVITED TO these meetings because, HONESTLY, they don't lead to ANYTHING.'

Towards the end of the conference, while political leaders from over one hundred countries stated their commitments to people and the planet, Greta had met more young climate activists, who, like her, were holding our leaders to account.

And they had an idea.

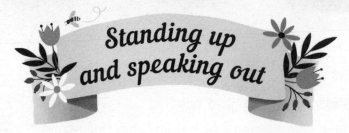

Standing up and speaking out

On Monday 23 September Greta and fifteen more climate activists headed to the UNICEF headquarters in New York.

'We are at the beginning of a

MASS
EXTINCTION

and all you can talk about is

MONEY

and fairy tales of
endless economic growth.

HOW DARE YOU!'

The youngest of the group was aged just eight and the oldest seventeen.

Ellen-Anne, Sweden

Raina Ivanova, Germany

Iris Duquesne, France

Raslen Jbeili, Tunisia

Carl Smith and Alexandria Villaseñor, United States

Deborah Adegbile, Nigeria

Catarina Lorenzo, Brazil

Chiara Sacchi, Argentina

Ayakha Melithafa, South Africa

They came together with an idea and the gumption to make it happen.

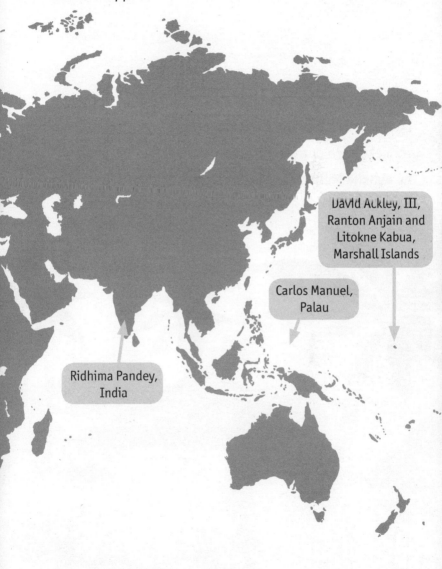

David Ackley, III, Ranton Anjain and Litokne Kabua, Marshall Islands

Carlos Manuel, Palau

Ridhima Pandey, India

They all have their own stories of how climate change has already **_impacted_** their lives, and they're determined to make sure our leaders know exactly how damaging it is. Ayakha Melithafa, who lives near the River Eerste, on the outskirts of Cape Town, South Africa, said:

'During droughts and heatwaves, people living in shacks don't have the luxury of turning on the air conditioner or cooling down in a pool. In extreme weather, those living in privilege are not the ones whose homes are flooded.'

Greta, Ayakha and the rest of their small but resilient group had restated the problem again and again. Now they were taking matters into their own hands. They planned to file a *legal complaint* against the five most polluting countries, and demand that they step up to their responsibilities.

UN CONVENTION ON THE RIGHTS OF THE CHILD

is the most complete statement of children's rights ever produced, covering issues like freedom of thought, belief and religion; right to privacy; access to information; juvenile justice and many more. You can read a summary of it on the UNICEF website.

If their petition was successful, the United Nations would state that the climate crisis is a CHILD'S RIGHTS issue, and push the five countries to do more to solve it.

Which were the five most polluting countries?

In 2019, at the time of the complaint, these were Argentina, Brazil, France, Germany and Turkey. Besides falling far behind on carbon-reduction targets, they support the use of fossil fuels to a point that doesn't fit with commitments like the Paris Agreement.

The complaint was filed with the support of the international law firm Hausfeld LLP and the environmental charity Earthjustice. Talking about the bold move, Michael D. Hausfeld, chairman of the law firm, said:

'Without transformational change in the next decade the human rights impact of climate change on the petitioners and more than two billion other children will be locked in and

IRREVERSIBLE . . .

What we all must do now is:

TALK LESS, ACT MORE.'

In Hausfeld Greta, Ayakha, Ridhima, Carl and the others found someone in power who supported their call for bold action. Together they're waiting for a decision, and the world is watching. There's much to be done, and Greta and millions more like her are up to the task.

The papers were signed, photos were taken, and the story went to the media.

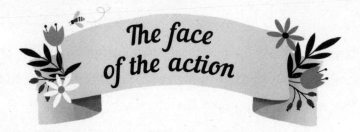

The face of the action

Greta was just fifteen when she became one of the most recognizable faces of the climate conversation. She refuses to be deterred even when she faces abuse, because when you're standing up for the future of our planet, of our home, nothing is big enough to stop you.

There's something else we can learn from Greta – never underestimate someone's strength. There was a time when Greta thought she was too small to make a difference; she couldn't find the will in herself to say the words those in charge would listen to. But then she did and the words came to her, so she stood and said them out loud.

The world is listening, and minds and actions are shifting so that the enormous crisis that is climate change can be solved.

Greta Thunberg is still a young woman, and this is a book about the extraordinary life she has lived so far. Now she's been joined by other young people who share her grit and determination to make things better. They're from all over the world, proving that no matter who you are or where you're from, you too can **make a difference** in the world.

They are on the brink of adulthood, of a career, maybe even raising a family one day. It's at this time in a person's life that many of history's movers and shakers have made their mark, and yet Greta and her fellow activists have already exceeded the world's expectations.

Now look to yourself –
imagine what you have

IN YOU

to make a

POSITIVE

CHANGE

in the world.

No one is too small
to change the world.

'We can't

SAVE
THE
WORLD

by playing by the rules,
because the rules have to

BE CHANGED.

EVERYTHING

needs to change ~
and it has to

START
TODAY.'

★ ## 3 January 2003

Greta Thunberg is born to Malena Ernman and Svante Thunberg.

★ ## 2011

Greta Thunberg learns about climate change after watching a documentary at school.

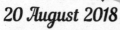

★ ## 20 August 2018

Greta embarks on her solo strike outside the Riksdag in the run-up to the Swedish general elections.

SKOLSTREJK
FÖR
KLIMATET

9 September 2018

Sweden's general election is held.

September 2018

Greta announces that she will continue her strike every Friday, and so the #FridaysForFuture movement is born.

☀ *30 November 2018*

15,000 students in thirty Australian cities take to the streets for their own #FridaysForFuture protest.

☀ *2 December 2018*

The United Nations Climate Change Conference opens in Katowice, Poland. Meanwhile strikes are organized by young climate activists in 270 cities across the globe.

15 March 2019

The first global #FridaysForFuture march is held, with 1.4 million people participating in over two thousand countries.

15 December 2018

Greta addresses world leaders at the conference.

14 August 2019

Following an invitation by UN secretary general António Guterres, to the UN Climate Change Conference in New York, Greta sets sail for America on *Malizia II* from Plymouth, England.

28 August 2019

Greta arrives in New York, following her fourteen-day voyage across the Atlantic.

23 September 2019

Greta addresses the United Nations Climate Change Conference. She joins forces with fifteen more young climate activists to sue the five most polluting countries.

20 September 2019

Greta leads the Climate Strike in New York City.

21 September 2019

The United Nations Climate Change Conference opens in New York, with over one hundred countries in attendance, to discuss progress on existing targets and set new ones.

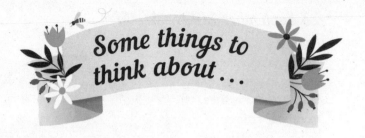

Some things to think about...

Greta Thunberg is constantly thinking of ways to help the planet. Can you think of everyday ways to be environmentally friendly?

Greta wants the world to know that no matter who you are, you can make a change in the world.

Is there a topic that you feel passionately about?

How would you convince the world to take notice?

Index

Quote Sources

Direct quotes throughout are taken from the following sources:

Page 11: 'Sweden is not a Role Model' (Greta Thunberg, *Medium*, 14 August 2018)

Pages 13, 24, 25, 48, 50: Greta Thunberg, schoolgirl climate change warrior: 'Some people can let things go. I can't' (Jonathan Watts, *Guardian*, 2019)

Page 19: 'Greta Thunberg: 16-year-old climate activist inspired international youth movement' (*Newsround*, 24 April 2019)

Page 43: 'Greta Thunberg Sets The Record Straight' (Steve Hanley, *Clean Technica*, 2019)

Page 45: Greta Thunberg speech to UN secretary general António Guterres in Katowice (3 December 2018)

Page 53: 'Swedish PR Guru Raised Millions by Helping Make Greta Thunberg a Climate Celebrity' (*Pluralist*, 25 September 2019)

Pages 57, 58: 'Australian school children defy prime minister with climate strike' (Bard Wilkinson, CNN, 30 November 2018)

Page 60: World Economic Forum (January 2019)

Page 62: 'Video: Greta Thunberg gives speech at the UN COP24 climate talks' (*METRO*, 2018)

Page 66, 76: @GretaThunberg Twitter, 31 August 2019

Page 68: @GretaThunberg Instagram, 31 August 2019

Page 78: Watch: Greta Thunberg sails into New York for UN climate change summits (*EuroNews*, 29 August, 2019)

Page 81: Video: We will make them hear us': Greta Thunberg's speech to New York climate strike (Reuters, *Guardian*, 21 September 2019)

Page 85: Transcript: Greta Thunberg's Speech At The U.N. Climate Action Summit (NPR, 23 September 2019)

Page 86: 'Greta Thunberg: Five things Greta said during her US climate change speech' (*Newsround*, 18 September 2019)

Page 89: UN climate action summit, New York (2019)

Page 93: 'Cape Town activist wants to teach climate literacy.' (Tammy Petersen, *news24*, 25 September 2019)

Page 96: '16 Young People File UN Human Rights Complaint on Climate Change' (Global News Wire, 23 September 2019)

Pages 102–103: 'The 1975: Greta Thunberg writes climate change essay for album' (*Newsround*, 25 July 2019)

The Extraordinary Life of
MICHELLE
OBAMA

Available Now!

Have you ever wondered what it takes to become one of the most influential women in the world? Find out in

THE EXTRAORDINARY LIFE OF
MICHELLE
OBAMA

Read on for a sneak peek . . .

WHO IS
Michelle
Obama?

$\mathcal{M}$ichelle LaVaughn Robinson was born in the South Side of Chicago, Illinois, in the USA, on 17 January 1964.

*M*ichelle's parents, Fraser Robinson and Marian Shields, were normal people, with normal jobs. Her dad operated pumps for the city's water plant and her mum was a secretary for a clothing company.

Growing up, Michelle shared the living room of her family's one-bedroom apartment with her older brother, Craig. Their room was split in half by a sheet hung from the ceiling so that the two children could have a room each. Craig and Michelle were so close that people thought they were twins, even though he was nearly two years older than her.

Michelle's family didn't have a lot of money so the one-bedroom, one-bathroom apartment had to be big enough for the four of them, but they definitely still enjoyed **treats** like pizza on a Friday night, while evenings and weekends were taken up with playing board games, reading books and seeing family.

Have you read about all of these extraordinary people?